RECYCLING, RE-USING, AND REDUCING YOUR GARBAGE!

ENVIRONMENTAL PROTECTION FOR KIDS

Children's Environment & Ecology Books

Baby iQ
Builder Books
EDUCATIONAL BOOKS FOR KIDS

Oh, my! Waste is everywhere!
We are running out of space.
We have to act now!

Kids, in this book you will learn some helpful ways to do proper waste management. Learn the 3Rs and know how they are done!

Your simple actions of proper waste disposal can make a difference! Recycle whatever you can. Produce new products from old ones. It can be a fun and an exciting activity.

HOW CAN WE REDUCE WASTE?

The best way to help the environment is by reducing the waste we are producing every hour, every day.

WHAT CAN YOU DO?

- Buy products with simple packaging that already contains the information you need on their labels.

- Use your computer to keep informed about what is happening instead of buying newspapers every day.

- When doing paperwork and research, print only what you need. Don't waste paper.

- **Buy only the things that are necessary or important.**

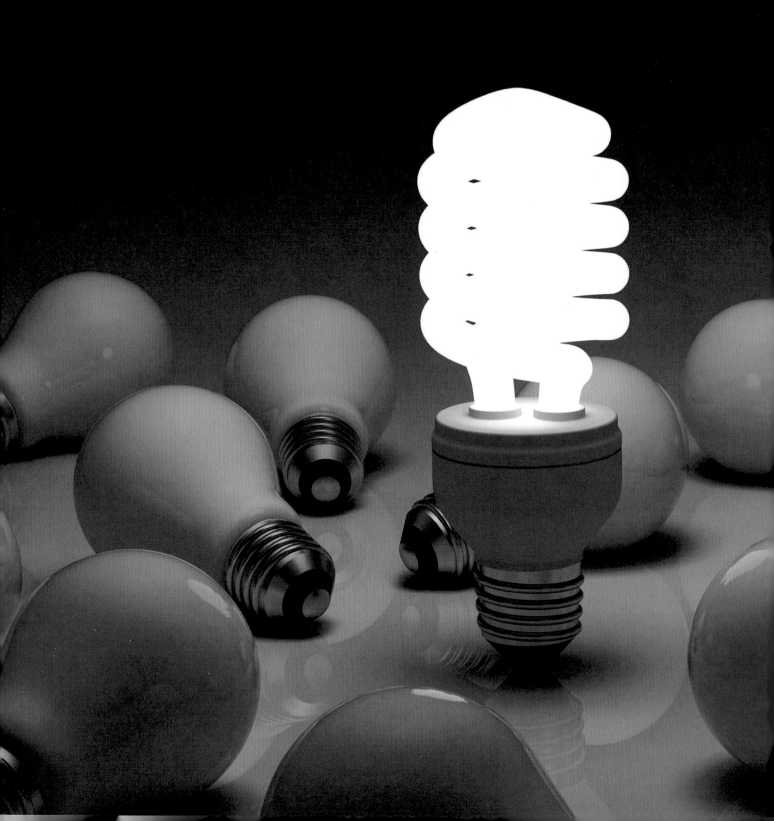

- **Save energy by turning off lights and appliances when you are not using them.**

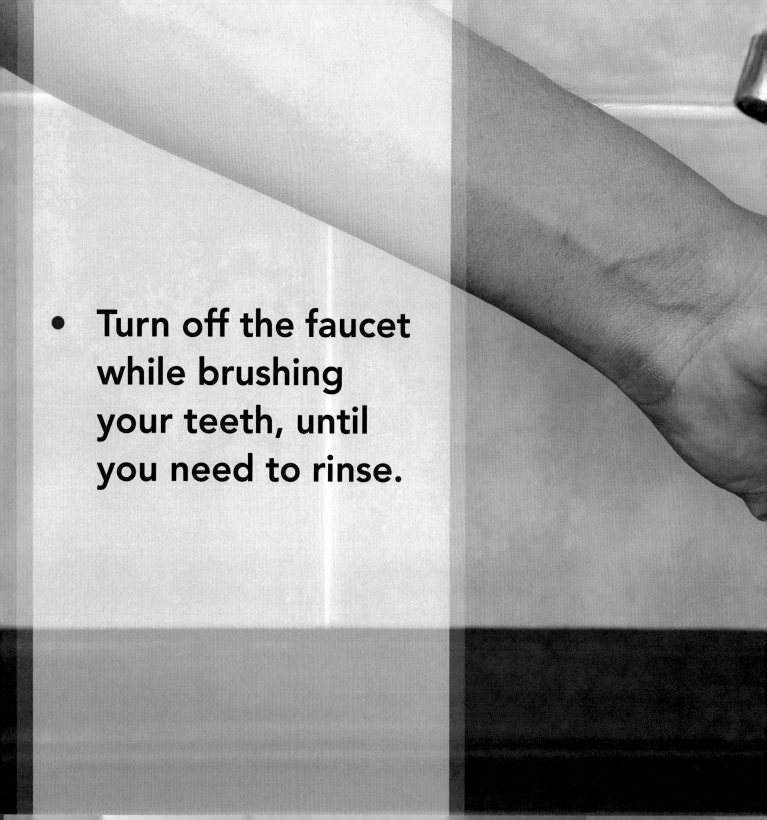

- **Turn off the faucet while brushing your teeth, until you need to rinse.**

- Take the bus or car pool with others. Walk or ride your bike instead of using a car. This will save energy and reduce air pollution.

HOW CAN WE REUSE?

Find ways to repair and reuse things rather than throwing them away.

WHAT CAN YOU DO?

- Make fun arts and craft projects from shoe boxes, coffee cans, milk cartons and other containers.

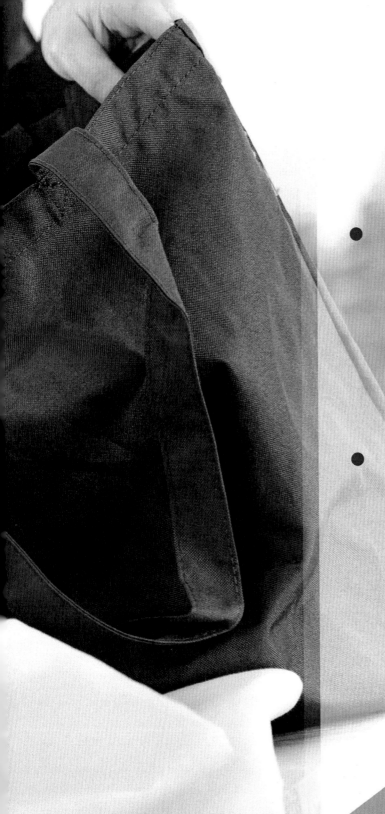

- Use reusable bags to take your packed lunch to school.

- Use reusable plastic containers as food storage.

- Give the things that you don't want any more to your friends or to a charity. These may include your old shoes, clothes, furniture, toys and many other things.

- Cloth sacks should be used when buying goods from stores. You can use them again rather than using paper or plastic bags and then throwing them away.

- **Don't use disposable plastic utensils when eating. Instead, use silverware and dishes.**

HOW SHOULD WE RECYCLE?

Get the valuable materials from things and make new products from these old things.

WHAT CAN YOU DO?

- Recycle soda cans, paper bags, and milk cartons. These things are made out of recyclable materials.

- Buy products that contain recycled material. These include paper towels, garbage bags, and greeting cards.

top 5 ways to reuse
this bag

① WRAP A GIFT IN IT
② FILL WITH OLD
CLOTHING & GIVE TO
THE NEEDY ③ SELL AND
DONATE TO A FOOD PANTRY
USED BOO STORE OR
THRIFT SH CH ④ CRAFT
PROJECT HAT, MASK, PUPPET,
PAPER AIRPLANE ⑤ USE AS
A TRASH CAN LINER AND
STUFF WITH RECYCLABLES

MADE OF
100%
RECYCLED
PAPER

Their labels contain the recycle symbol which indicates whether they are made from recycled materials or they can be recycled.

- **Bring aluminum cans, plastic grocery bags and other recyclable things to recycling centers in your town.**

Reduce, reuse, and recycle!

The 3 Rs will help lessen the amount of waste that people generate.

Since most waste is non-biodegradable, the 3 Rs can do a lot of help.